Giving You The Best That I Got.....

with Fire & Desire......

Shanda Cuthbert

BookLeaf Publishing

India | USA | UK

Dedication

Preface

Acknowledgements

1. New Poem

Seven days doing nothing with you.
Six hundred four thousand, eight hundred seconds, spent
making love to you.
I can spend another seven days doing nothing with you.

2. New Poem

Smile from your heart.
Love from your soul.

3. New Poem

You're bright as the Sun,

and dull as the Moon.

Roses are red and Love is too.
Violets are blue, like me without
you.

Love me like a dog and I'll be
your best friend.
Treat me like a bitch, and I'll bite
ya like Mike.

4. New Poem

Brave is the bold who
Love without tears.

Brave is the man who

dreams without fears...

5. New Poem

She's the woman in a
love song.
You're the man women
cry about.
Endless streams of tears
falls like Niagara.
An un-watered flower,
the petals wither away.

Fertilized in dirt, watered
in spit.
The hug-less child
bloomed to be, the
concrete rose.
She rose from the dead.
Nurtured her soul,
watered her roots, with
sunshine & soul kisses.
Kisses from the top of her
head, to the ball of her
feet.

*She's the woman in a
love song.
You're the man she don't
seek.*

6. New Poem

Your absence has caused so much

joy.

Your presence always felt like a
volcano erupting.

7. New Poem

Once upon a time I believed in happily ever after.

Prince charming and fairy tales.

Knights in shining armor.

Then I met you.
Fire breathing dragon.
Spoon fed poison,
masked as love.
Led me down a rabbit
hole, and it's off with my
head.
Kissed another toad
dressed as prince.
Evil as stepmother,
wicked as witch.
No one to save me.

The tales we tell.....

14

8. New Poem

Somewhere between the
sunset and sunrise I fell
in love with you.
Maybe it was the
brightness in your eyes
when you talked about
your dreams.
Or the calmness in your
voice when you consoled

me.
Definitely the spirit of a king you exude within.

Sometimes when I look in your eyes, I see the child in you.
Sometimes when I look in your eyes, I see the fears in you.

Sometimes when I look in in your eyes, I see the pain in you.

Sometimes when I look in your eyes, I see the love in you.

But, most nights when I look in your eyes, I see the God in you.

Share your time with me.
Share a song with me.
Share a dance with me.
Share your soul with me.
Share your spirit with
me.
Share a prayer with me.
Share a life with me.
Share a stone with me.

9. New Poem

Stung by a Scorpion caused
much pain.
Tingling and numbness.
An electric shock through my
body.
I cant breathe.

I can't speak.

I can't see.
Vaginally injected his venom, the
stinger went deep.
Touched my soul, awaken my
heart, changed my life forever.
This crab is no match for the
scorpion.

10. New Poem

Stop pushing me away.
Stop acting like that.
Stop sending me to
voicemail.
Stop blocking my calls.

Stop texting me.
Stop calling me.

Stop peeking through my window.

Stop stalking me.

Still in love with me?

11. New Poem

Suddenly the sun hit around a
quarter to six.
Staring in your eyes, there was
no surprise.
Saw another you with no visons
of me.
See visions of me, with only
visions of me.
Suddenly the sunset around 2006.

12. New Poem

It's not easy loving you.
I watch you in awe as
you reminisce, lost in
memories of lovers past,
like a child on Christmas
morning.
I marvel at your

admiration for them. You appreciate their curves, the fullness of their lips, captivated by beauty woven in melanin. You trace the contours of their bodies, feel the strength of their plight. Your heart dances with stories of their inner thighs, reliving moments of passion.

Your voice trembles with
memories of her sweet
grip. Eyes frozen in
flashbacks, a soft lullaby
when you speak their
names. A harem of souls
frozen in time.
I listen intently, no
judgment, just fear.
How can I become all
these women in my 5'3"
frame, when their essence

dances so confidently in
your mind?
Here I stand, small yet
fierce. Worries curling
like smoke in the air.
Will I ever measure up to
those who once laid in
your bed?
Each moment you recall,
each moment of bliss.
Will I ever be the
masterpiece revered in

the gallery? The key that
unlocks the entrance to
your heart?

In this chaotic tapestry, I
weave my own thread,
Love as my canvas, hope
as my paint.
And I wonder, will your
heart truly be mine?

13. New Poem

My soul was drawn to you from
the moment I sat down. My
subtle advances went unnoticed,
until the time was right.

Immersed in your presence,
mind, body, and soul. The
connection is clear a current
unseen, yet strongly felt.

I see a reflection of my own
longing, A mirror of desires,
hopes, and unspoken schemes.

The world melts away when our
hands intertwine, leaving only
the warmth of your touch and
the silent promise of something
more.

A love I crave, a need I can't
deny.

With every beat of my heart, I
feel you near.

My soul is drawn to you, where passion remains.

14. New Poem

*I always get dealt the same bad
hand.
Full of possible's and useless
diamonds.
This crimson hand bleeds red,
devoid of heart.
No spade to find a King, no
Queen to wear her crown.
A fool I was to trust that Jack, a*

dream deferred when the Ace
emerged.
My partner's diamonds, cubic
and worthless, a glimpse of hope
turned to shame.
A Joker knocks my partner out.
Now I'm stuck, another casualty
in loves cruel game.

15. New Poem

I wanted to be better for him when his critiques felt like a pastor's weekly sermons, inspiring me to greatness.

I knew I loved him.

When I felt no need to defend my independence, but willingly submitted to his guidance.

I knew I loved him.

No longer a captive to the Strong
Black Woman trope.

I knew I loved him.

When I held my tongue to silence
the nitpicks.

I knew I loved him.

When I trusted his leadership,
not mistaking it for dominance.

I knew I loved him.

When he trusted me to lead on days he stressed, unfazed by my strength, because I knew my position.

I knew I loved him.

16. New Poem

I come to you pure, pure
as the day I was born.
Clean hands, body, and
soul.
The remnants of the past
washed away, down an

empty drain with
indiscretions and used
souls.

I come to you pure, arms
open, heart healed.
I give myself to you, to
have and to hold, till
death do us part.

I come to you pure, my
sins washed away, no
trace of others.

Others with cruel
intentions that sparked
my insecurities.

I come to you pure, pure
as the day I was born.
I'm not afraid to love you,
just afraid you won't love
me back.

17. New Poem

I admire and envy you.
Let's dispel the myth that
envy breeds hate, that
jealousy is formed.
In the glow of your light,
I find my reflection.
Admiration wrapped in a
sweet little tension.

While I stand in your
shadows, cheering from
afar.
It's not jealousy lurking,
its love on the rise.
A sisterhood bond, a
connection that ties.
I envy your courage, the
strength in your stance.
The way you own the
room, the way you take a
chance.

Our ancestors are proud,
as you break through
barriers, fill the spaces we
belong.
There's no shade in my
spirit, no hate in my
heart.
Sis, lets uplift each other.
In your success I find
strength that is mine.

18. New Poem

A Sunday kind of love.

Sunday football, Sunday
sex.
Your favorite Sunday
cologne,
Smells like Tabacco
Mandarin.

Smells like Love.
Sundazed on Sunday's

is a Sunday kind of
LOVE.

19. New Poem

The very thought of losing you feels like a wooden stake to my heart.

Eternally killing every memory of you, of us. Your love bite over powers prudent thoughts.

I'm right back where I
started.
Bound by your love.

Your wife knows.
I see it in her eyes
I feel her rage, I feel her

fears.

Your wife knows!
I see it in her eyes.
I feel her pain, I feel her
tears.

Your wife knows!
I see it in your LIES.

20. New Poem

I would've said I love yesterday,
But, feared I wouldn't say it
again tomorrow......

9 years

8 months

7 weeks

6 days

5 hours

4 minutes

3 seconds

2 do it all again with U

1 last time.

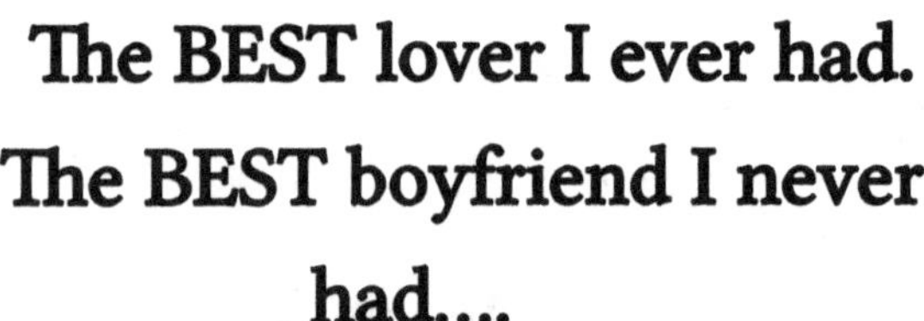

The BEST lover I ever had.
The BEST boyfriend I never
had....

21. New Poem

I'm the tobacco on your lips, the whiskey you sip. Macallan 18, sweet and warm.

Smokey filled room, with

a pinch of me.

Fishnets & High heels.

I'm the lipstick on your

dick that makes you cum

quick....

www.ingramcontent.com/pod-product-compliance
Lightning Source LLC
LaVergne TN
LVHW021242200726
843509LV00012B/1569